LOVE OF RAIN

PRITILATA NANDI

I would wholeheartedly wish to dedicate this book to those amazing people
who accomplished great things during their life, but never gained a sense of
recognition and popularity in our society.

This book is dedicated to my daughter Arundhati, my dear parents and some
special people whom I miss alot.

Contents

Contents

Foreword

A young Indian woman, Pritilata is a professional teacher and a passionate author. This book comprises short realistic stories representing the various strata of societies we live in, with fictional characters playing their part actively.

Preface

This book has some realistic stories which highlights the realms of society enlightening the audience with values such as empathy, love, care and kindness. It has been composed in really simple english dialect for enhanced readability and making it accessible to everyone from every strata.

The author wishes everyone a happy reading session valuing the love of rain that makes all the lives worth living.

Acknowledgements

I would like to express my humble gratification to my daughter, Arundhati for inspiring me to start my blog and now we are a family 1585 members strong at Wordpress! Feel free to follow my writing at 'Endless Dreams and Boundless Imagination'.

I would like to extend my gratification to Sougata Mazumder who helped me throughout my blogging journey. Credits to Soumik Sinha for the creative art behind the lens, the photograph used as the cover picture of this book.

Last but not the least a very special thanks to my brother Ashish Kumar for helping me in the entire publication process.

CHAPTER ONE

RAINBOW

This morning is cloudy, last few days Mithai is doing a morning walk around this park. It is near to her old locality where she was born and brought up. She came here from America for selling her parent's house. Suddenly she sees Sona is also walking there. She tries to avoid him. But Sona calls with her name," Ei Misty"(Misty is Mithai's nickname both means sweet). How are you?"Mithai stops, she hears her sweet nickname after a long time from her Sona da. In the meantime, Sona comes near to her. Sona says, "Let's sit there on the bench". Mithai becomes surprised she thought her Sona da will never forgive her. They talk about their current situation before leaving he says "Misty are you free today? Then come to my place for lunch".Swapna my wife, Titli and Joy my children will be very happy. Okay bye, I have to go to the market for chicken, I know you like chilly chicken and fried rice very much. We will wait for you". Saying all he leaves the place.

Sitting on the beach Mithai sank in her 35 years ago sweet memories. Then she was a student of class ten. Sona was a science teacher of classes ten to twelve of his coaching Centre in the same area of Mithai. The students called him Sona da. He was about 25 years of young, handsome and a very attractive guy with excellent results. But he wanted to be a private tutor. At every event of their locality Sona was the leader of all, maybe it Durgapuja, Kalipuja or Holi festival. Mithai was the only child of her parents, ambitious and very good at studying. After passing class ten she took science and started taking tuition from Sona's coaching Centre. Slowly

Mithai got attracted to Sona but Sona never took her seriously she was like his other students. His ignorance made Mithai madder at him. Then the mobile phone was not so much available so she wrote love letters and put those on his table under some book. In every letter at the end, she expressed that, she will die without him . Sona da made her realise to think properly but she was adamant. Slowly Sona also became weak to her.No one knew about their affair. Sundays were their outing day Sona gave her ride on his bicycle and both enjoyed it a lot. They often visited fairs or parks or markets and ate puchka, pakoda, chilly chicken fried rice together. Sometimes Sona bought yellow bangles or earrings for her. Days passed by with their romantic love. It was a rainy Sunday, they were sitting together with catching hands and were talking in this park after rain they saw Rainbow in the sky making a bridge through the earth to heaven. Suddenly Mithai kissed him on his lips and Sona hugged her tightly that was their first kiss. They both became colourful with their Rainbow love they promised they will remain together forever. The Rainbow was the witness of their beautiful love. After passing class 12 Mithai got a chance to read engineering in a different city. There she met Rohan as her college mate, Rohan was a scholar. One day he proposed Mithai. Then Sone was out of her sight so her mind changed from Sona to Rohan within a few days. She realised Rohan is perfect for her. In front of Rohan, Sona was nothing. In her last letter, she wrote to Sona that, she did a mistake, a private tutor will never be her good choice. Sona felt empty and cried a lot with those love letters as if his world became to an end. Mithai ignored Sona as she was in love with Rohan. After married Mithai went to America with Rohan. Then Sona also married Swapna.

It was slightly raining and Mithai comes with a bunch of yellow roses to Sona's house. Yellow is Sona's favourite colour. After lunch, the rain stops and a beautiful Rainbow appears in the sky. Sona, Swapna and Mithai sit together on the balcony to see the beauty of nature. Then Joy calls his mom, Swapna goes to his room. Then Mithai catches Sona's hand and says. " Sona da please forgive me. I got punishment for my betrayal. I ran after a standard but never got so much happiness in the small things of life which l got from you, Rohan is good but very professional, I love him but never got that essence of love. I got a big house, cars every luxury of life but never got that love which l desired. I missed my Sona da a lot with tears". Listening all Sona says," I also missed my Misty and her adamant attitude. I have forgiven you many years ago because I loved you madly, your aggressive love taught me the meaning of love. Love is nothing but sacrifice. Swapna is very good but she never sat on my bicycle like you or behaved so adamant like you And I am grateful to you because you first showed me my standard and that's why I took the job". Both were feeling the same pain.Sons says" Misty you are my Rainbow on the sky of my heart I kept you hide a secret in my soul forever".Mithai says," Sona da you are also the rainbow of my first love, let's both do one promise maybe we could not get each other in this birth but in our next birth this two souls certainly will meet and make Rainbow between the earth to sky".Both's eyes fill with tears. Only Rainbow is the witness again.

CHAPTER TWO

COLOUR

Today is Holi, the festival of colour. In this Spring season, the Holi always brings happiness to all. On this day people become colourful like Nature. From the morning the Bengali people play Holi by spreading different colours to each other. In the evening they enjoy this day with sweets, delicious foods and various drinks. But this special day brings tears to Pamela's eyes. Though she doesn't get too much time but try to cook one special recipe for her children and friends but doesn't touch any colours. She left that day around twenty years ago from her life. One of that day made her life colourless. Holi only memories her red colour.

Pamela falls in love with young Tarun, son of a cloth shopper from a middle-class family. She was from a very rich family. She knew that her parents never will take Tarun as their son in law. From the first day, Pamela realised Tarun's endless love for her. Pamela didn't see any status only felt the enormous love of Tarun in her heart. He was so mad at her that he could do everything for her. They often met each other secretly. After a few days, they decided to be together. So one day they fled and got married. Tarun promised her that, he will work hard to make her happy all the way. After five years of fighting, he took his father's business at some position. Then Pamela became a mom of two children. Tarun loved Pamela so madly and felt very proud to get her as a wife. He involved Pamela in his business and told her that, except for business he is going to open a small clothing company in her name. So they can manufacture various kinds of dresses. On an auspicious day, he opened a clothing company in the name of " Pamela clothing and trading". It was his dream to make Pamela feel proud of him so that she never thought that, she made the wrong decision to marry him. Their love story and business were going smoothly. For Tarun Pamela was his fortune and for Pamela, Tarun was her God. They were so in love madly. Pamela found herself a lucky one to get Tarun in her life. No one day had gone without kissing her, Tarun went to his work. They never made a little argument ever. Their adjustment was perfect. It was a special day for Holi Tarun planned to take her for an outing. In the morning they played Holi with each other with children and in the evening Tarun took her on his bike and went to a restaurant. The evening party was just begun there. All were very happy but suddenly there started fighting between two people for some reason. Suddenly one of them shoot with a gun and the bullet hit Tarun's head. He fell to the ground. Pamela took his head on her lap, his red blood and her tears made her wet. Before death, he said to Pamela that, he will always be with her and also said to look after their children and the business.

Since then Pamela started fighting, her life became dark suddenly. But she never give up and always felt as if Tarun was beside her. Tarun means sun in the light of the sun she makes her strong and overcomes all odds. The colour of Tarun's love gives her new strength to become a successful businesswoman. For her efficiency and as a woman entrepreneur, she got various prizes, not only that she opened a new brother company in the name of " Tarun gents wear". Maybe Holi has gone from her life but her company makes people colourful with various kinds of dresses.

CHAPTER THREE

FIGHTER

Aniket Barma is going to Publish his new book on his life ," My dark world". Though he already has written lots of popular books. Some of his students , his mom Renuka Barma and some of his colleagues and the publisher are present in the function. After his little speech his mom catches her loving son Anik's hand and help him to get down from the stage. Renuka's eyes fills with tear but she feels very proud on Aniket.

Renuka had some critical physical problems, before Aniket she got pregnant for three times but due to miscarriage she didn't become a mother.And then she gave birth Aniket at her seven months of pregnancy. All thought he will not survive even the doctor also lost hope but after spending two months in the hospital's neonatal intensive care unit he came to his house. His dad Anirban named him Aniket that means one who makes the world his home. Aniket was very sharp from his childhood. Once Anirban got a big amount by selling his village property but that night some robbers came to their house,when they were threatening Anirban and Renuka to handled them that money then suddenly Aniket told one of the robber," Uncle I know you , I saw you on my school way".Hearing this that man at first shot Anirban and then Aniket and they fled away. Anirban died at that moment. Aniket survived but his optic nerve damaged severely. So he lost his vision parmanently.

Aniket started fighting from then. His beautiful world became dark suddenly. Everyday he cried in pain ,he wanted to see but he couldn't. When someone showed him sympathy he got angry, he shouted. His mom hugged him and said," Anik, you are my big fighter, from your birth you are fighting, now you have to live in this way, forget your past, except your present quickly, and fight hard.".Slowly he tried to overcome the situation. He got admission in the blind boys academy. He learnt braille. He finished his master's and then he joined as a teacher in a popular blind school. He always inspires his students saying his life story. It is more pathetic for one who suddenly becomes blind than a born blind.He chose a blind lady as his partner. Now he is a popular teacher, author. Not only that he has founded a blind school and donets a big amount for the development of blinds at his school and both of them work for the blinds from heart.No,his story is not so famous like Helen Keller but he is a born fighter. Many people don't know how he fought during his life. He never give up only hard fighting was the aim of his life.

CHAPTER FOUR

PROMISE

Today is Rakshabandhan day. A very special day for brothers and sisters.There is a specific time when sisters tie a sacred thread or amulet around her brother's wrist to symbolically protect them from all evil and offers sweets and gifts. In exchange, the brother offers her gifts or make some commitment towards her well being. Every year Payel takes leave from her office on this day and goes to nearby slum area and ties Rakhi to some of the boys there and tells them about her brave brother.

Six years before it was a special day of Rakshabandhan. Then Payel was 21 and her brother Sourish was 18,a young courageous man, always tried to help others in their need that's why ,all loved him very much. Their dad had a grocery shop and mom is a homemaker. After graduation Payel started working in a factory as an accountant to help her dad. She was working there last siix months.The factory was not so far from their house. Her duty ended around at 8 PM. Everyday Sourish waited at the gate of the factory and then both brotherand sister returned home home together on foot.From the morning Payel was very busy to arrange for the Rakhi and then she had to go to the factory. It was Monday so the factory was open. At the right time she tied a beautifulflowerRakhi on Sourish wrist with a full plate different kinds of sweets and also gave him a costly shirt as gift. Then she spread her hands and said, "Bhai give me my gift". Sourish said, "Didi (elder sister) what are you saying! You know I am a student. From where I can get money to buy a gift for you? After finishing study I will do a big job then I will give you ,what you want? But now I promise I will protect you from all kind of peril ". Payel said, " Ha ha really! You know you are three years younger than me. You will save me"! Sourish said," Yes didi I promise I will ,till my last breath". Hearing that Payel kept her palm on his mouth and said ,"Don't say it again please.My Rakhi is to protect you from all evil and you are saying about death"! And then after finishing all she went to the factory. In the evening when they were coming back to home ,on the way four drunkard men suddenly started teasing, thinking them boyfriend and girlfriend. They were useing slang languages also.Payel knew her brother will not tolerate all so she started walking fast but then one of them pulled her scarf (dupatta). Sourish attacked the man and hit him hard and fell him down then he ran after another one who was trying to abused Payel. Sourish kicked him but suddenly one of them shot Sourish with gun, seeing Sourish bleeding they fled. Payel was shouting for help. Some boys of nearby slum came hurriedly and took Sourish hospital but he didn't survive.

The next day the news came on the various newspapers, in the pressure of opposition party the state government was forced to gave Payel a job. Her dad also died within one year in the grief of his only son.After her loving brother's death every year on this Rakshabandhan day she goes to different slum area not only to ties Rakhi but in return she makes the young guys promise to respect the women like their sisters so that ,no sister have to loose her bhai so pathetically.

CHAPTER FIVE

PARASITE

Anand Bakshi is a retaired school teacher. He lost his wife five years ago. His son is in Mumbai and daughter is in Bangalore. They both are well settled. Last fifteen days he is coming to the pension office to clear his pension. But the employees of this department always delay in their work. While he is waiting a peon comes to him and takes him to the officer's room. Seeing him the officer comes near to him and hugs him. Before he says something the officer says, "Anand Bhaiya have you forgotten me"? I am Krishna . Anand," O my God! Krishna! What a pleasant surprise! You become so young and big I didn't recognize you! How are you? Anand ," I am well. How about you?I have taken the charge of this office from yesterday. I have joined today". Don't worry your pension will be clear within a week.I know here the employees are deceitful. That's why the government has sent me here. Look at that person waiting there he was the officer in charge for last fifteen years before me .He retaired one month's ago now he also has to come here about his pension". Think the situation !he had created!. But now I have to make everything normal". Then they both talk to each other for a long time about their life. Now Krishna has his wife and a son . They both take their phone numbers. Before leaving the office Anand requests Krishna to come to his house on next Sunday. Krishna says, "Anand Bhaiya you are my big brother. Im always grateful to you. You know today also I write your name as my local guardian. I must will come with my family and you also has to come to my house. You know how much I missed you! After my class twelve I went to your house to find you but it was locked." Anand," Yes after my mom's death I sold that house. Krishna I also called you again and again on that last day of village. Where were you"? Krishna," Bhaya I was so sad I was crying under the cot . I saw everything and after your leaving. I came out.". Anand ," Ha ha ,Really! I thought you got angry on me". But now on the weekdays we will meet together and try to get back our old days." Krishna," Yes Bhaiya sure".

On the way to home Anand was thinking how he met Krishna about 35 years ago. Then Anand was twenty five years. He got a job as an assistant teacher of a government village school. There he was given an old mud house with two rooms to live. Krishna was a six years old orphan boy. He worked for Anand ,brought water from the hand pump, cleaned the rooms.Helped Anand in cooking in return of meal. But Anand started him teaching in his off time. Not only that he got him admission to a primary school and became his local guardian. Anand loved him very much because in that remote village Krishna was his only companion. Krishna also was very fond of him. He called Anand 'Bhaiya'. Days were passing by. On the vacation Anand took Krishna to his home. Anand can remember when he fell sick once how little Krishna took great care to him. He brought medicines from a local doctor, whole night he sat near to his head,gave him medicines,fed him. Always Anand said Krishna, " Listen try your best to become a good person. Don't show others your weakness. Keep faith on yourself.One day you will be a successful one". After six years when Krishna was in class seven in Anand's school then Anand transferred to an another school. Krishna didn't want to leave Anand, he requested him to stay there. Anand tried to make him understand that it was not in his hand but little Krishna became very upset. A new teacher was appointed for the school. Anand wrote a letter to that new teacher with request to take care of Krishna's education. At the last day Anand wanted to give him some money and a new sets of dress to Krishna but after calling again and again he didn't find out him. So he left a letter with some money and dress on the cot and went out.

Suddenly Anand's phone rings , Krishna is on the other side. Krishna says" Bhaiya can you come today in the evening. The government is going to honoured some officers for their good work I am one of them so I want you to be present on that function. He sends a car for him. After getting reward from the minister the announcer requests Krishna to say his feelings. Krishna shows an old letter and read it loudly. " Krishna my brother Iam going. Some new one will come. But you don't spoil your life for no one. Don't live like a parasite. If you have immense concentration then you can hit a target. So keep focus on your target." Bye take care. Anand". After reading the letter Krishna calls Anand on the stage hugs him and introduce him as his big brother and says, "Today Iam what, only for this person he told me not to be a parasite I only follow it". A happy and proud feeling just touched Anand' s heart.

CHAPTER SIX

MONALISA

Monika is a Hindu girl and Lesia is a Christian girl. They both are very close friends from their childhood.They are neighbours. They both studied in the same school. Now they are college students. Monika is doing honours in English and Lesia in Mathematics. They are good in study. Their parents are also very good friends. In Durga Puja Monika gives gift to Lesia and in Christmas Lesia does the same. They go to everywhere together whether it is movie or coffee shop or restaurant or shopping mall. The two families had gone so many places like Kashmir, Gangtok, Simla together. Monika's dad Manik, has his own autoparts business and Lesia' s dad , Jhon is a service man. Monika has an elder brother,her mom is a homemaker. Lesia is the only child of her parents. Her mom has a beauty parlour. Monika's nick name is Mona and Lisa is Lesia's nick name. From their childhood they like to spend time with each other.

Now they both are eighteen years old. They both are beautiful to look. Monika is not so fair like Lesia. But she is very attractive. Monika is a good dancer and Lesia is a guitarist. Now a days they feel as if they will not live without each other for a moment. When they remain in their home they continue text to each other. They both go to college by Lesia's dad's car. In the college a young boy Sohan, likes Monika very much. He wants to propose her. But Monika doesn't feel anything for Sohan. Actually the boys never attract her. She always feels something for girls. On the other hand Lesia also has the same problem. Usually we human being are attracted by opposite sex. But for Monika and Lesia the matter was different. They are women in body but feel for another woman. They both were confused. They didn't know what to do? They were very shameful for it. One day Sohan holds Monika's hands and said her ," I love you Monika" in front of some friends. Lesia was also there.Hearing this Monika started laughing. Seeing that suddenly Lesia got angry on Sohan without any reason. She became very upset. Monika noticed that. When they were returning from college Monika asked Lesia,"What happened to you"? Why did you become so serious in the college"? Lesia replied, " Nothing, you don't need to think, go and get your boyfriend Sohan and enjoy his company". Monika didn't know what to say? She said ," Listen Lisa I don't like Sohan . You are more important in my life than Sohan". I don't know what has happened to me but whole of the day I just think about you". Hearing this Lesia answered, " Mona I am also facing the same problems. If you can mind that's why I didn't tell you anything. But when I see you with some others laughing,I feel very lonely". Please don't leave me alone". They both fall in love with each other.

It was a rainy day Lesia's mom and dad had gone outside for some work. Lesia called Monika at her house. As they live near so Monika went there without an umbrella and she became wet by raindrops. Lesia gave her a towel to dry her hair. They both touched each other. A strange feeling came into their body. They hugged each other tightly and started kissing madly. This is the first time they felt as boyfriend and girlfriend. Their new journey started from that day .This news they didn't hide for a long. Their parents tried to make them understand that it can will destroy both of their life. Even they restricted them not to meet each other for a long time but nothing could stop them. They understood that they were made for each other. After five years Monika's parents arrange to get her married that day they both fled. No, their life was not so much famous as Monalisa. But after a long fighting two poor girls Mona- Lisa started living together.Though they lost their own but didn't leave each other. All were not in their hands but people abused them without realising their problems. Mona- Lisa showed two women can also make a family without men. 'Mona-

Lisa' suffered a lot in their life that's why they promised to help them, who are like them under a charity name "MONALISA".

CHAPTER SEVEN

SYMBIOTIC

Mridula is a middle aged woman. She had a small and beautiful family with her husband Samir and only son Tirtha. They had a confectionery shop in a big shopping mall. Dad and son both ran the business together. Their shop had a goodwill. The shopping mall was situated in an aristocrate area. Their business always was in good profit. There were six workers worked here. Tirtha was then twenty five years old. He was a very handsome young man. Mridula took great care of her family. She is a theist. So every early morning she spends around two hours worshipping her God and Goddess. Her family specially her son was her world. She was very happy with all. She had nothing to wish to God. Life was very easy for her. All were going smoothly. But suddenly one evening a fire had broken out in that shopping mall. It was started by a short circuit. The shopping mall was a five storied building. The fire rapidly spread out of the whole building. There was a delay in the start of rescue operation. So about forty people died in the fire. Tirtha was one of them. More than 200 firemen and 40 fire tenders were involved in bringing the blaze under control but the lack of adequate fire fighting equipment were major factors that contributed to the blaze out of control. Almost all the shops and offices were destroyed fully.

It was so sudden no one could imagine it. Poor Mridula not only lost their shop but also their only child. Everything became dark for her. She tried to kill herself. Life became meaningless to her. After hearing the news she became unconscious. Then only tears left in her life. Whole of the day she cried with the name of Tirtha. She didn't know what to do? She became very sick. Her relatives, her own, her husband try to make her understand to forget everything. But she couldn't. Mridula wanted to adopt a child but Samir was not agreed for her health and looking at her age. Doctor advised Samir to change the house to get rid of Tirtha's memory. Samir moved to his village home. Mridula was so sick that she was not able to cook or doing anything. That time they got a very poor married Muslim woman Masum as their maid servant. First Mridula was not agree to appoint her for her caste But then Samir made her understood that She needed the job and she is very good. She called Mridula 'amma' and did everything for her. Masum lived with her husband,who has an another wife and three children. Samir started a grocery store here. Within few months Masum became very fond of Mridula. Mridula also looked her as her daughter. Slowly Mridula was doing well. One day Masum said to Mridula," Amma There is a good news. My pregnancy test has come today it's possitive". Mridula answered, " Really ! Don't worry I will take care of you and your child".

After six months Masum's health became deterioting. She was suffering from anemia. Her husband didn't take proper care of her. He had not good earning. There was always a quarrelling between his two wives. Only Mridula and Samir tried their best to keep Masum well. When Masum was ninth months pregnant one day she requested Mridula," Amma promise me if I die you will raise my child". Mridula said," No, don't say this . Nothing will happen to you. You are my daughter so your child will be my grandchild.We will always take care of our grandchild". Masum said that to her husband also. After fifteen days Masum gave birth to her daughter Munni. But her condition became very serious and she couldn't survive. Now Mridula and Samir adopt Munni as their daughter with the help of local police. Masum's husband also doesn't not oppose. Little Munni becomes her own child to Mridula as Tirtha. Mridula again finds meaning of life after getting Munni. Whole of the day she starts to remain busy for Munni. Little Munni helps her to fade Tirtha's memory. And Munni also gets her parents to love her and raise her.

CHAPTER EIGHT

WARRIORS

Today Mukesh is going from this village with his wife Rumela. He has got his transfer to another bank. He came here around six years ago as a branch manager of this village bank. Then Rumela was not agreed to come here. She is from a metro city. She has to come here only for Mukesh. She didn't want to live without him as then she was newly married. Before coming here Rumela was doubtful about her, she thought that ,she will not stay long in this village but now she doesn't know how she has passed six years here. Lots of villagers have gathered here to say them' good bye'. Specially women, everyone is tearing for Rumela.Some of them have brought some handmade gifts for her. She says them with her moist eyes" Hey, why have you brought all? I don't need any gift.I have got your love that is enough for me". One of them, Karuna answers," Don't say it Rumela Didibhai,(Didibhai means elder sister). You don't know how much we are grateful to you.Before you,we didn't know the meaning of life".Tutu says, "Didibhai before you, our life was boring,we were very much dependent on our men, now we can breathe freely". "You have given a fresh breeze in our life. Don't you know RumelaDidibhai? Amina says. Rumela feels very happy hearing all. She hugs all of them and then she takes all the gifts and sits in the car.Their car slowly starts moving leaving the villagers. All of them raise their hands to say 'Ta Ta'.

From the car Rumela looks out of the window ,she feels that the village ,the roads are very much familiar to her.She never thought in her imagination that, these illiterate or little literate women will become so much close to her or will give her enourmus love. When she first came here everything looked her dirty. Whole of the day Mukesh stayed busy with his work. She felt very lonely. Then she started roaming through the village with her maidservant Karuna and used to take lots of photos in her digital camera. From Karuna she knew the bad condition of the women. They were very much dependent on their husbands.And the men didn't give them any values.She talked to Mukesh about them. He advised her to do something to make them self-sufficient and in this way she will not feel lonely. She saw most of the women can make various handmade things from bamboo strips for their home use. This gave an idea to her. One of her friend has some big shops of handmade gifts items. She first discussed it with her friend. Her friend agreed to buy those items.Then She called a meeting with some village women and said them everything

The women were very happy to know her plan. Rumela formed an association with seven very skilled women in the name of. "THE AMEZING THINGS OF BAMBUSA".The women after finishing their household work started making different bamboo products. First few months it was going slowly for insufficient investment. Rumela arranged a loan from her husband's bank. Not only that she appointed two trainers from city to trained the women. After training their items became more beautiful. The women are very hard working. Now around hundred women work under this association.They have learnt how to keep daily account, how to calculate profit? How to send the goods in the city etc etc. Now their goods go to different cities.With the help of Rumela they become not only self sufficient but their life style also has changed.Their husbands also feel very proud of them.The women have brought revolution in that village.sometimes Rumela calls them warriors.

CHAPTER NINE

FERTILITY

Reshmi has fallen seriously sick. Last fifteen days she is suffering from fever.She is very weak. Her husband Abhi is not here.He has just return back to his work one month ago. He is coming. Reshmi -s in-laws don't take too much care for her.They didn't want Reshmi as their daughter in-law. Only for their son Abhi,they were bound to take her in their family. She is from a poor family. Her dad is a farmer of a village, Palashpur. Sundari is a small river there in that village. On the river side people used to come to do picnic in the winter season. Reshmi sometimes went there with her friends in the afternoon to catch the beauty. Once Abhi and his friends went there for picnic. That day they both saw each other and it was their love at first sight. Reshmi is very beautiful with long hair and Abhi is also a handsome young man. That day they only smiled to see each other.After that day Abhi went to Palashpur for many times to visit Reshmi.Those days were so beautiful for both of them. Only for Reshmi, Abhi started playing guitar again and Reshmi concentrate on her singing. Generally Abhi went to meet her on Sunday. Then mobile phone didn't come to market. So whole of the week they both waited eagerly for each other. They both understood loving is so beautiful. Whole of the day they remained happy to thinking about each other. They smiled alone. Abhi is a government employee. They realised they will not live without each other.They dreamed about a happy life together.

After one year Abhi's parents wanted to get him married and they started looking for a bride for him. But Abhi told them about

Reshmi. Abhi's parents had nothing to do but didn't become very happy .They started their new journey with fun and enjoy. But after three years their life started changing slowly in the pressure of reality.Abhi's parents wanted their grandchild but it didn't happen. They and some of relatives started blaming Reshmi for not having any child. Abhi also had a wish to become a dad. For this reason they both argued with each other and it brought a misery in their life.Abhi took Reshmi to a doctor but it didn't work.In the meantime Abhi got transferred to different city.He planned to take Reshmi after setting everything there. Reshmi requested Abhi to check up himself for their baby. Abhi and his parents had a belief that,a man never can be infertile and it's very shameful for a man to check up.

After Abhi's gone Reshmi became so lonely. Her in-laws didn't like him .Most of the times she cried for Abhi. Now loving became so painful for her.She didn't take food properly. She neglected her health. Sometimes she didn't want to live anymore. She thought she never will be a mother so she wanted to get him rid for her. After six months Abhi returned back for fifteen days. Reshmi was so happy.That fifteen days just go very quickly. Abhi told her that he had gone to a doctor and the doctor said he has faults.That's why they had problems to become parents. But the doctor gave him medicines and hope everything will be good. Abhi returned back to his work. But he has to come back and admitted her hospital .After checking her doctor says the good news that, she is going to be a mother. But she needs extra care. All become very happy to hear the news. Abhi tells his parents and the relatives that men also can be infertile so it's not right to blame women for childlessness. Reshmi didn't have any problem all the problems were in him.

CHAPTER TEN

DNA

Roselina now lives in Houston in America with her husband Jhon and two children Alis (18)and Jishan(16). It is a beautiful city. This city is known as the world capital of space exploration. She is very happy with her family. She loves herchildren very much But sometimes she feels very sad when she trys to memories the love of her own mom. Before Violin's death she told her that, they adopted her from India from an orphanage home . Then they had no child .Violin and Sam were young couple, when they realised they never will become a parents then they adopted Roselina from that orphanage home .But after few months they got separated.Sam married again. Violin also started a new family and had her own children .Yet Roselina stayed with her. From her childhood Roselina didn't get mom's love properly though Violin loved her very much. Now sometimes Roselina thinks to search her own mom from India only to asks her," Why did she leave her"?

So Roselina comes to India. She visits that orphanage home. It was around forty five years ago. Then Roselina was only one year old. The authority of that home open their old book to find out the old list of the baby,whom they gave to Sam and Violin. It was then not computerised, manually written. After a long search they get the name of the girl. Then Roselina was Krity and her mom' s name was Kamola. There she finds out the address of her actual mom. She goes to that address but it was fake. But she doesn't give up. She starts searching near by areas with the help of that orphanage home not only that she takes the help of the newspaper. After few days an old woman comes to her and says her that she is Kamola's sister Bimala and also says her everything about Kamola. Kamola was then 18 years old. She became pregnant before marriage. Then it was an offence. Our society doesn't accept it easily. So in fear of the society she had to leave Roselina in that home .Now Kamola lives in an another area. Roselina goes there and meets her mom Kamola. They hug each other and start tearing. Her husband had passed away. Her only son doesn't look after her.

Kamola doesn't let her go to the hotel where Roseline stayed after coming to India. Seven days Roselina stays with Kamola. Kamola cooks everything what she likes to eat. Though her financial condition is very poor. She introduce Roselina with the neighbours as her own daughter. Whole of the day they talk to each other, at night they sleep on the same bed by touching each other. Kamola talks to her in english not very well like Roselina. Roselina enjoys the company of her mom very much what she didn't get ever. Her take careing mentality, her love just make Roselina forget her sorrow. Before leaving India she does DNA test. Unfortunately it shows negative that means there is no blood relation between Kamola and Roselina. May be the DNA test becomes negative but for her Kamola's love is real mom's love. During the week she never felt it was artificial. She thinks in her mind what does DNA say that doesn't a matter for her, mom's love and Kamola is more costly than anything. Science defeated by humanity.

CHAPTER ELEVEN

SUCCESSOR

Mallika Sen is a widow, now 65, who lives alone in a two-storey big house made by her husband in Kolkata. Nowadays she is suffering from some health problem, she doesn't walk well. Rea a young lady takes care of her very much and calls her mom. Mallika is living only for Nik, Rea's son.She loves Rea as her daughter and Nik is her life.Her two elder sons are well-established and live in different cities with families. They don't get time to visit their mom. Last four years they both have shown much ground for not coming to Kolkata. The last time they came here after their youngest brother's death. Mallika's youngest son Tridib is no more. He was a military man. Four years ago in the border war, he passed away. Then he was in Kolkata with his mom for three months of leave but suddenly war started and he had to join one month ago and gave his life, became a martyr. After that incident, Mallika became sicker. She couldn't take Tridib's death easily and lost all hope of life.

Tridib was a young, handsome and tall man. From his childhood, his dream was to join the Indian army. His mom never wanted it. At the age of 20, he got a chance to serve the country as an army man. At that time he loved Rea a beautiful young lady in his locality. Rea lost her mom a long time ago. They were classmates. Two families were well known about the affair of Tridib and Rea. They thought about their marriage also but unfortunately, Tridib's death destroyed everything. Then within a few days, Rea's dad arranged her marriage though Rea did not much agree with it. She loved Tridib madly. She got Tridib for a few days but those beautiful days of love she couldn't forget.She had to do it in the fear of society as she was about two months of pregnant then. After the marriage of seven months, she became the mom of her son Nik. After giving birth to Nik Rea and her husband had started adjustment problems as Rea's husband doubted the fatherhood of Nik. Then they got divorced and Rea came back to her dad.

When Mallika knew everything about Nik she understood Nik is her Tridib's blood. She brings Rea and Nik to her home and adopts him as her grandson. Nik brings a new life for Mallika. Little Nik is like her Tridib. She can't think of herself without Nik.He is her joy, her happiness and God's blessing in her life. Her two elder sons left this city a long time ago. Then Tridib was her everything. She realises that she has to do something for her Tridib's blood so she calls her two sons saying that she wants to distribute her all assets. Hearing this her two sons come immediately. When she asks them who is going to take her responsibility both of them deny it, saying that they have no option as they have to run their families. Mallika announces that she doesn't need them, not only that she is going to give half of her assets in the name of Nik as he is not only her successor but also the only source of light in her life. Rajib and Sanjib become surprised about her decision.

CHAPTER TWELVE

HEART

Dr Arya Sirker is a famous cardiac surgeon in this city. He works in a Government hospital. He has a happy family with wife and only son, Arjun he is also a medical student. Dr Sirker is very popular for open-heart surgery. Till now he has done lots of operations successfully. Tomorrow he has to operate on two patients. So in the evening before leaving the hospital he was reading the medical history of those patients. The junior doctors look after the patients before the operation, he only does the surgery. Suddenly one name looked very familiar to him. Lata Bose, the name took him to his teenage memory.

Arya Sirker was a student of A. K . Memorial school. It was a co-education higher secondary school. He was very naughty and not good in Mathematics but always scored the highest marks in biology. In class ten they got a new Mathematics teacher LataBose, a very beautiful young lady in a serious mood. All the students were afraid of her as she didn't like any inattentive students in her class. She was very strict about maths. In her class, every student must have finished homework, otherwise, they got punishment. She always praised those who tried to do good in her subject. After every exam, she always gave some gifts to those who scored above 80% and encouraged them for doing better. Her teaching technique was very unique. So the students always remained aware of her toughness and tried to do their best. She was a very good teacher for those who were good at maths. Arya didn't like her for the first few months because she always scolded him very rudely. He thought she was heartless as she punished the naughty students without thinking about their prestige in front of others. He called her 'Ragi mam'.(Ragi means hot-tempered) . One day it was a cricket tournament on the school ground between class ten and eleven students. One of the students hit the ball so hard that it stuck fielder Arya's forehead and injured him, blood started flowing then Lata mam came running and did the first aid and took him to the nearest hospital with some other school staff. She waited there till his parents came. During that time she didn't leave his hands for a moment and continuously said to him," Don't worry Arya, you are my brave student, nothing will happen, you are going to fit in again within a few days". He was crying in pain but his scary mam's touch gave teenage Arya an unknown feeling of happiness in his heart. After that incident, Arya became one of her good students and he also tried to do his best in maths for his ragi mam. She became his first crush, and ragi mam became loving mam. After passing ten he took science and he knew Lata mam will take maths for class eleven and twelve also. Only for her he took mathematics as an additional subject. Those beautiful three years Arya passed by seeing and thinking about his beautiful mam. He kept his first love secretly in his heart. He didn't say anyone about his feelings. After passing twelve he went to a different city to study medical.

Dr Sirker goes to see the patients and becomes surprised to see it was really his Lata mam with white hair and looking old and tired. But her face is still beautiful like earlier. She was sleeping, when he touches her hands she gets up. He tells her that, he is Arya and she recognises her student, Arya. Her tears start rolling down from her cheeks. Arya takes her hands into his hands and says, " Mam don't worry you are going to be fit again". Lata says, "Arya, I am feeling proud to get you as my student. I heard your name as one of the topmost cardiologists 'Dr. Sirker' but never thought you are that, naughty Arya whom I once missed a lot after you left school". Hearing that Arya's eyes fill with tears. He also missed his mam at that time. He thought those feelings were only his personal, but he didn't realise his mam also had the same. Sometimes Some unknown attractions work between two human hearts which we call in the name of 'love', that sometimes make us insane or crazy.

CHAPTER THIRTEEN

ENTREPRENEUR

"Rekha you go to Balligunge, Deepa, you visit Dhakuria that old patient, Namita, you have to go to a new house in Saltlake, Amina wait sometimes for clients phone ". From morning Binita remains busy with a phone or giving instructions to her staff. All the staff are women here. They are mostly illiterate or little educated. But without them, our society will not run smoothly. Binita's office is well decorated. Her laptop is full, with the whereabouts of her staff. Their addresses, phone numbers, photos everything has been kept safely in her laptop. Not only that, she has a website for her company. The women are very grateful to her as they can earn and run their families with her help.

Binita Banerjee is now 55. She has started this business around twenty years ago. Manish is her husband, they have one son Biman and a daughter Maya. Then Biman was 10 and Maya was 6, suddenly Manish became seriously ill. Then he worked in a private office and Binita was a homemaker but she took nursing training, after passing class eight. While coming back from the office Manish met an accident and his right leg was seriously injured. He became bedridden and he was forced to leave his job. The doctor advised that it will be a long term treatment to stand again on his feet. Binita didn't understand what to do? How to run her family? Manish had small savings but within a few days, all were finished. Her children were small and how could she work outside leaving bedridden Manish? After the accident, she got help from her friends and relatives for a few days but then she understood they were not much happy to help her. She realised their ignorance. Often she cried alone and eagerly wanted to find some way to arrange food for her children and husband. She understood what hunger meant? She started thinking to do something from home as she had no option. She got nursing training so she went to some nursing homes and talked to the authorities about the availability of jobs. She realised the nursing homes need some helping hand workers. First, she went to some slum areas to collect some women who need jobs. Then she started sending those women to those nursing homes in some conditions. Slowly more women joined in her centre. They work at home as domestic help, in the office, in nursing homes.

She started with two nursing homes now her Centre supplies these helping women throughout the whole city not only in the nursing homes but different houses as domestic help also. Around thousand of women work under her "B.B. Helping Hand Centre". In her office, her representative also remains busy the whole day with clients phones about where they have to send the helping women. B. B. Helping Hand Centre is a very famous and reliable company in the city. Now Binita has become a big entrepreneur. Now Manish also has cured. He also helps her to pay the salary of the staff and looks after the financial matters of the company. Few women work a daily wage basis and a few monthly salary basis. Her son is now a doctor and her daughter works in a bank. Once she realised the suffering of starvation now she is the person who has spread her hands to help those women who are not well trained or literate and save them from appetite. The journey was not so easy for Binita but she never give up. Lots of poor and helpless women find the meaning of life joining to her centre. Binita shows us if you have a strong desire in mind to do something you can. She feels proud of herself as a woman that she has done something for the society and the women like her.

CHAPTER FOURTEEN

ROUND

Anupama Banerjee is very happy today as she is going to fix the marriage date of her only son Akshay with Rehana Akthar from a Muslim family. After a little later they will go to Rehana's house in North Kolkata. Anupama is from a Brahmin family but a very receptive woman, now she is 60. The last two years after her husband's death she came from London and resides here in India(South Kolkata). Her son Akshay still lives in London. A long time ago she was forced to go to London and there she got married and had her family with Tarun Banerjee also was from Kolkata. When she first time heard about Rehana she was surprised. Akshay and Rehana both studied at the University of London and fall in love. After five years of their relationship, they decided to get married in Kolkata at their origin. Anupama already met with Rehana in London and liked her very much. Rehana is a scholar and very beautiful to look at.

When their car starts going to that lane of North Kolkata towards Rehana's house Anupama feels that the road is very known to her. Though she went away from Kolkata around thirty-nine years ago. After reaching Rehana's home she realises that this house once belonged to her though it becomes bigger. Rehana is the youngest child of her parents. Her dad died four years ago. Her two elder brothers have a business of cybercafes throughout the city. As Rehana is a very good student and got a scholarship that's why she went to London to study. Her family did not much agree with this marriage but her mom Sakira Begam didn't listen to anyone.

She only looks after her daughter's happiness. There was a photo of Rehana's dad Rajiv on the wall when Anupama sees it her eyes filled with tears. All the memories of her past come in front of her eyes.

Anupama was then 21. She took admission to one of the computer Centres of North Kolkata to learn computers. It was in the name of' Rajiv computer Centre'. Rajiv Akthar was the teacher and the founder of that centre. Within a few days, Anupama Chatterjee fell in love with young, handsome Rajiv. It was a beautiful love story. They started watching movies, eating at restaurants going on long tours by bike and wished about a happy life together. One day her dad saw both of them on Rajiv's bike. Anupama knew her powerful Brahmin dad never will accept her relationship with a Muslim guy. So that day they got married in a temple and Rajiv brought her to this house. She stayed there only for two days as his wife. They thought to take a photo together as husband-wife but it didn't happen. On the third day, her dad came to Rajiv's house and said he wanted to arrange a marriage party at his home and invited Rajiv and his parents to come and take Anupama as his wife with full Bengali rituals. She trusted her dad and leaving Rajiv she went back to her home with dad. But that day her dad forcefully sent her to London at her uncle's house and threatened her "If you try to go against it I will kill Rajiv". That was the last day she saw Rajiv. She was so mad at his love, she sacrificed her love for his good. Then mobile phones didn't come to India only land phones were in a few families. She didn't make any communication with Rajiv ever. She cried a lot to forget him but didn't erase him from her heart forever. Again she came back to India with her husband and one-year-old son after ten years but didn't try to meet Rajiv. She kept her love hidden secretly into her soul. The marriage date of Akshay has been fixed after fifteen days. Anupama and Sakira hug each other. Sakira says," My husband Rajiv loved a woman madly at your name that's why I didn't get him fully ever. He never tried to do any harm to that woman but cried very often. He believed in sacrifice in love. But I promised my daughter to make her happy so that she doesn't have to suffer like her dad". Anupama stands speechless only tears roll down through her chicks. She understands that the same story happens again, but this time her son is able to get his love. She feels very happy and proud to think that the earth is really round.

CHAPTER FIFTEEN

FIELDER

Namita Murmu lives in Sundarban with her husband Arjan and two children. Her inlaws are very old they also live with them. Arjan is a fishmonger. Very often he and his three partners go to catch fish in the sea by a troller. Whatever they catch after selling, the four partners take the money equally. The money is not enough for Arjan's family. So occasionally he goes to sea with his wife Namita to catch fish so that he can be able to earn a little more.

Namita is from a poor family but very hardworking and courageous. She liked to play cricket. She wanted to be a cricketer. She used to play as a fielder. Her coach very often said her Jonty Rhodes. As she could easily hit wickets by throwing the ball. But she couldn't continue it for her poverty. She always has regret for it. Her dad was a farmer and her mom a homemaker. When she was 23 her parents arranged for her marriage to Arjan from the next village. After the wedding, she came to Arjan's house. They both love each other very much. Arjan is the only earning member of his family. So it was very tough for him to meet ends. Though Namita didn't know anything about fishing but only to help Arjan she learnt everything about fishing. At the time of the lockdown Arjan and his partners were not able to go to the deep sea to catch fish. So very often Arjan and Namita started going to catch fish in the sea by their small boat. There is a deep mangrove forest on the two sides of the sea. There very rarely people have seen the Royal Bengal Tiger.

One day Namita and Arjan went to catch fish with two other friends on their boat. When they were busy catching fish at the seaside suddenly a tiger came and attacked Arjan and dragged him to the forest. Namita didn't know what to do? She jumped with bamboo from the boat and started beating the tiger, other two friends also took bamboo and did the same. The tiger was pulling Arjan very aggressively seeing that, Namita took her chopper which she always takes with her and threw it into one of the eyes of the tiger as a great fielder and it hit the tiger's eye. Out of the pain, the tiger left Arjan and ran into the forest. though he became unconscious. Arjan came back from the hospital after one month. Only for her, Arjan got a new life. She got a prize for her bravery from the government. All praised her for her courage. Maybe she didn't become a cricketer but only for her excellent fielding, she saves the life of her loving husband. That gives her peace of mind.

DEBT

When Promila sees the news of Sumita on the front page of the newspaper, with her photo with the Chief Minister, Promila gets surprised. She knows Sumita very well. She is not a famous person she is just a beggar. One rainy day she came to Promila's big house begging and then Promila heard her life story. That day Promila was alone in the house. Her husband is a big businessman, was out of the city, and her only son studies abroad. Suddenly the rain started heavily, Promila didn't want to give Sumita shelter in her house as she was doubtful with unknown Sumita but due to rain, she was forced to call her. Sumita waited there for around half an hour till the rain stop. Then she told Promila that she didn't know about her parents, husband or children or any relatives. Even she couldn't memories her past. She only knows she is a beggar. Promila thought maybe she is mental and lost her memory and went out of her house and didn't return. Sumita also told her now she lives in a slum area near a railway station. Promila gave her an old sari and ten rupees. After that Sumita came three or four times but Promila didn't feel good. As if it was a burden for her. Now she thinks she did a great mistake.

Promila goes through the news. The Chief Minister praised Sumita and said ," You are the richest woman from the heart I have ever seen in my life. I am proud of you. I don't know what to say to you? If only thirty per cent of people have the same mentality as you then there will be not so much division in our society. Now I can promise you, from today you don't need to beg from door to door, we are going to give you a job as housekeeping staff in a government hospital. The reporter asked Sumita," How have you done this"? When you are a beggar? Sumita said, "Actually I know the sufferings of poor and helpless people. Throughout my life, I only take from people, from society. I have seen lots of people in my life. Except for few people, most of them treated me with hate. They just threw two, five or ten rupees to me when they have too much, sometimes some people closed the door in front of me. But I didn't mind as it was the last way for me to live. But few people take me as a human being. We all are the debtor to our society as we take all the facilities from it. So I wanted to free my little debt to society. That's why I saved money slowly. After the flood when I heard that, people are donating to the Chief Minister Relief Fund I wished to give my whole life of savings of rupees 3 lakhs. The local councillor arranged all. And the Chief Minister called me here in the office."

Once this news not only surprised Promila but also all of us. If a beggar can give her all savings! why don't we help others a little as human beings if we are able? We all are indeed the debtor to our society so we need to release us from the burden of debt.

CHAPTER SEVENTEEN

TIGER

Bishal Nandi has arranged a marriage ceremony function with the help of local club. Five girls from poor family are going to be married together. Not only this year, he is doing this last few years.He takes all the expense of marriage alone.He gives fifty thousand rupees to each couple as gift. When the poor parents bless Bishal his eyes moist with tears in happiness. He knows his parents suffering after their daughter's marriage. He thinks about his past what he was ? And what he is now? Now he is a big one in the society and once he didn't get enough food.

Bishal was born and brought up in a very poor family with his three siblings,two elders sisters and one elder brother.His dad was a farmer, mom homemaker. His nick name is Bagha (tiger). There were not any good school in their village so most of the students leave their study in the middle and started working in the field. Girls were getting married at early age .There was only one school which was upto class eight.After passing class 8 Bishal didn't stop study as his elder siblings. He got admission in a city school where he went by bicycle to save money. His dad sold his farm lands for his daughter's marriage. Then he worked in others field to run his family and that time often they remained hungry. Cycling was very taugh for Bishal.After coming back from school he became very tired. One day one of his sir asked the students, what did they want to be? Bishal didn't know what to say ? So he replied," Sir I want to build my own school so that,no one have to go through the pain of long hour cycling".Sir was silent for a moment and then he said," If you have that strength for doing it then I will think,you a real tiger". He took the challenge into his mind and started dreaming about his school.

After graduation he started his first school in the name of Swami Vivekananda, with ten students taking two rooms in rent. He appointed two female teachers and a menial staff for his school. He started working as a hawker of chocolate , biscuits etc to earn money to run his school. Once he didn't pay rent about five months the landlord locked him in the room and threatened him," From today I will finish your dream parmanently". After few hours one of the female teacher Swati gave all the pending money by selling her earrings and freed him. Later he married Swati. After a long struggle he bought his own land and builded a primary school and named it Swami Vivekananda Academy. Now it has five branches, two of them free primary school, two secondary school and one higher secondary school, around 1200 teachers and staff work in his school.He never pay any attention to his family or children, school is all to him. He always lead a simple life. Really he has proved he is a tiger.

CHAPTER EIGHTEEN

RED

Daya Das is 32, works as a domestic help in Routh's family for few years. She lives with her widow mom Mina and a little cousin brother Sanu. She is a married woman but her husband left her as she couldn't become a mother. She thought herself an unlucky woman in the world. Sisir and Bina Routh have only son Prakash.He is 16 years old. Sisir is a big marchent of clothes. Daya loves Prakash very much as her brother. From his childhood he has breathing problems and he is very weak as he was born with a small hole in his heart.Its called septal defect. The doctor suggests to a surgery to cure it parmanently. But there is a big problem as his blood group is O Negative which is one of the rare blood group ,he can only receive O Negative blood.But this group is universal doner that means he can donate his blood to any group.

Mina and her husband Jadu got Daya twelve years after their marriage. They left all hope to became a parents.They were the adorer of Lord Krishna. When Daya was born they believed it was the grace of lord Krishna so they gave her name 'Daya' means kindness.Jadu was a daily wage labour and Mina a homemaker. From her childhood Daya is very soft hearted. After sudden death of Jadu Mina became helpless then Daya started working as a domestic help.Mr and Mrs Routh were very much anxious about their son Prakash as doctor told them to arrange blood for him during his surgery. They tried hard but couldn't do anything. Daya saw them sad ,she wanted to know what had happened? After knowing all she said to Bina," Amma, I will donate blood to my brother Prakash , don't worry". Bina said," Daya it's a rare blood group how can you help us? Do you know your blood group"? "No amma." Daya replied.When they didn't arrange from anywhere then they test Daya's blood just casually but surprisingly she has also O Negative blood group.

Daya's mom opposed against her decision to donate blood in fear that she will fell sick. But the doctor told them that a woman can donate blood once in every four months. And it's a noble work and it doesn't harm our health anyway. The doctor makes them understand " Safe blood saves lives", and he also said Daya is going to save a life by doing it. Then she donates blood to Prakash and saves his life. Now she is one of the member of rare blood group and not only Prakash she saves lots of lives with her blood.When someone gets well she feels proud on herself now she thinks she is one of luckiest woman in the world. She campaigns and inspires women to donate blood. Now there are lots of members in her group and they are always ready to donate blood.She never thought that her name can ever come in the Newspaper. When a reporter asks her,"What inspires her to do it"? She replies," We all are human beings may be with different castes, language, food, dress, nationality, religion etc,but if we judge ourselves by blood then we will find everyone has same colour that is red. I only see this red colour nothing else to save life".

CHAPTER NINETEEN

AEROPLANE

Kulsum Soren has taken her eight years old son Kanu to the hospital. The doctors have said if she did little late then may be they will not survive him. She thanks the doctor and also the God again and again. She doesn't know how she had done this? The hospital is about twenty km far away from the health centre. Her husband Hasu works in a different city and comes here twice in a year. Kulsum stays with old in-laws ,a sister-in-law and her only son in a remote village. She has lots of things to do,whole of the day.After finish- ing household work she has to look after their paddy field.Now it's Rainy season in this time many poisonous snakes roam here and there. When Kanu was bathing inthe pond he felt pain on his big toe of right leg and showed his mom,she understood it was snake bite.His toe became red and was bleeding. Kulsum immediately tided his toe with a slim cloth and took to him to the local primary health centre.The nurse said it will not possible to treat him there she needed to take him to the hospital soon. It was raining heavily.Kulsum did not get any vehicle to take Kanu to the hospital.

Kulsum came to a poor family, she is the youngest of her five siblings. She was not good at study but very good at sports. Their physical education teacher loved her very much. She was the best runner among all the students. No one can bet her in running.Wherever she went to play she got the first prize. Her teacher and friends called her 'aeroplane' as she ran very fast. Her teacher requested her parents to take care of her this talent. She needed healthy food and good training. But due to their poverty they didn't do anything for her. When she was eighteen they got Hasu as their son-in-law. Hasu works as a fourth class staff of a private company in a different State. So they got her married with Hasu. Then she forgot all her talent.

When Kulsum didn't get anything to take Kanu to the city hospital she started running putting Kanu on her shoulder.Then only one thing was in her mind to reach the hospital as early as possible. She was running and running tirelessly. She memorised her days in the school when she was called aeroplane.Inthe meantime Kanu became unconscious. In between running she was crying and praying to God to save her child. Within fifty minutes she came to the hospital. The doctor quickly gave him antivenom and save him.Hearing all from her the nurse and doctor became surprised. The doctor says " You can easily bet Usain Bolt ". Yes, she doesn't know the name of the best runner in the world or has not got any gold, silver or bronze medal but she only wanted to save her child and that was more important in her life than any medal.

CHAPTER TWENTY

ALTERNATIVE

When Ruchira was five years old her mom suddenly died. Her dad didn't take this shock he took a transfer to another city leaving small Ruchira in the care of her grandparents. After two years her dad started a new family there Ruchira was not allowed to join. Her dad didn't show any interest in her. She always missed her parents' love. Her grandparents were everything to her. They were quite old so she became very responsible from childhood. She never wished for anything costly from them as she knew her grandpa run the family with his small pension. She always felt happy with very little. She often cried for mom and prayed to God to send her to mom. She wanted her dad and thought to herself that, one day she will do something great and that her dad must realise how much she loves him. Whenever she saw someone with parents her tears came out. Grandparents knew everything but were helpless. One day her grandma advised her to write everything in a diary to decrease her pain. From that day she started writing about every moment of her life. It became a habit of her. Time passed by. Then she got married and after a few years, she lost her grandparents also.

After married she went with her husband to his workplace. Then She was a homemaker and She had not had many things to do there. So in the off-time, she expressed herself in her dairy. One day she saw an advertisement in the newspaper, they wanted small stories from new writers to publish in their newspaper. She thought to herself that she will try to write. Without saying anything to her husband she wrote her childhood story by pseudonym and sent it to the newspaper office with a phone number. After one month she received a call from the newspaper office and they wanted to meet her. She went there they told her that they want to publish her story serially if she can write. They offered her money. She never thought about it. She wrote everything to get rid of her sorrow but that missing valuable love motivated her to become a writer. She accepted it and she started writing her story in a very simple way with her experience and it became highly popular. She forgot her mom but with her imagination and feelings, she wrote for those orphans who are unlucky to get their parents' love. Later her husband knew everything and became very proud of her.

Now Ruchira a mom of two children is a renowned story writer. The Publishing Company published her first serial story as a novel and introduced it at the book fair, and lots of copies were sold. The first book she devoted to her dad. Her dad also read that novel. He understood his guilty. Not only that she donated her grandparent's house to an NGO for orphan children and named it" The God's children", and some percentage of her books royalty goes there every month. Once a week, she spends the whole day with those children like their mom, as she knows there is no alternative for a child beyond of parent's love. Only love is that special thing in life that inspires us to do everything.

CHAPTER TWENTY-ONE

GUILTY

Ravi works in a bank and his wife Anju was a teacher. Ravi is from a Brahmin family and the only son of his parents, Anju is from a general caste. It was around nineteen years ago when Anju was only 23 and Ravi was 28. They both went to their workplace by the same bus. From there their love story started. When they realised they are made for each other they said everything to their families. There was no problem with Anju's family. But Ravi's parents didn't want their daughter in law from the general caste. They opposed but Ravi was determined to marry Anju. They got married without the permission of Ravi's parents and started living together. In angered Ravi's dad cursed Anju that she will never be happy as she stole their only son from them.

After two years of marriage, Anju got pregnant. She gave birth to their son Arjun. But when he became one year old they understood there are some problems with him. He didn't speak or hear anything properly. He was different from other children. His growth was slow even he didn't do anything by himself. They became worried. They took Arjun to the doctors but there was no hope. They became depressed. Their happy life was going to worsen. Their relatives and friends became curious about Arjun as if they are very sympathetic to them but not. It hurt them badly. Anju only tears and Ravi always tried to make her understand everything will be right. Then they tried to get him admission to the school but no school gave him a chance. They advised them to take him to a special school where the disabled learns. They took him to one of those schools but it was not so satisfactory to them. Anju started thinking maybe it happened due to the curse. She always felt guilty for it.

They decided to do something for these disabled children so they can get proper care and sympathy and can think they are not a curse for society. They have also the full right to live in society. They both founded a school for those different kinds of children in their home in the name of "Mom's care" inspired by Stephen Hawking with only one student that is Arjun. Anju left her job and started working as a teacher. Now their school is one of the famous schools for different types of children and Arjun has passed class ten with good marks. Now they feel there is nothing to fear from the curse or feel guilty only have to decide the right path.

CHAPTER TWENTY-TWO

EVERYTHING IS POSSIBLE

Rukmini is a cancer patient. Throat Cancer. Doctors don't see any hope. But she is very happy. Now she has got the company of her special one, once she desired him as her husband. Now she can die peacefully and her last wish is going to fulfil. He always looks after her, gives her medicine, feeds her, takes her to the doctor and sometimes takes her to the fresh air. Once Rukmini thought to live together but didn't get a chance. After twenty-five years of long waiting, she has got it now.

Rukmini was a professor at a university. Was very attractive, humble, soft-minded. She was a spinster and lived alone after her parent's death. At her university, a young man got admission. Priyam is from another city. From the very first day, Priyam got attracted to Rukmini. Whenever she came to class Priyam looked at her constantly. She was just a role model to him. Within a few days, he fell in her love. Though there were about nineteen years of age differences between them. Every day Priyam waited near her place as it was near the university to say her something. But didn't get the courage. He also lived as a paying guest near the university. One day when Rukmini got out of her house he proposed to her with a rose "I love you". Rukmini was stunned she never thought in dreams it could happen. She started laughing. But Priyam was serious. He said he couldn't sleep well, eat well or study well only for her. The whole of the day she comes to his mind. Rukmini tried to make him understand it's never happened in the world and what society will say? But Priyam said," It will happen now and I am not afraid of society". Rukmini didn't understand what to say? just ignored him. Day after day he provoked her and said he will not live without her, but she took it casually. In the meantime suddenly she got seriously sick. She needed to admit to the hospital and Priyam helped a lot. Every day he visited her at the hospital and after coming back he took great care of her. During this time her mind slowly became soft on Priyam. She realised Priyam truly loves her. So their love story started, it was so exclusive. Rukmini just flow away with Priyam. She forgot her age the boundaries. They lived in different places but every evening they meet each other. Not only that, Priyam forced her to put sindur on his name and said after getting the job they will get married. He promised that he will never leave her hand. They both started thinking of them as husband and wife. They were so happy, it was an unexpected experience for both of them. Rukmini started loving Priyam madly. After finishing study at University Priyam went back to his city. First few months they talked to each other over the phone then she understood how Priyam was ignoring her? One day he told her that he did wrong, he couldn't marry her due to society. Rukmini was speechless. She cried a lot, became depressed. Her all dreams broke suddenly. She only said, "I thought you as my husband and you always will be. Only one last wish now is in my mind that," I want to get you at my death bed" Then everything stopped between them.

After twenty-five years one day, Pryiam called her over the phone and said he wants to visit her. Rukmini did not oppose she also wanted to see him again. After coming back Priyam told her he lied, he fall in love with Amrita who was his age. Then they got married but they always had an adjustment problem. After fifteen years of fighting, they got divorced. He always missed Rukmini's love for him. He begged Rukmini to allow him to her life again. Now they both are living together at Rukmini's house happily ignoring the fear of society. Now Priyam Crys secretly and is waiting when Rukmini leaves his hand, while once she cried and wanted to catch his hands forever. Actually, everything is possible in life.

DIPA

DIPA ,a famous production house for T.V serial.It is the 'light' house for the new comers and the old artists as it shows new vision to them,because the owner Parni Singh has a passion to work with them. Lots of Mega serials run with great TRP rate from DIPA.

Dipten Bose was once a hero of movies but after 45 he didn't get enough work in movies so he started working in T.V serials. Then he had two daughters and wife. At that time he was working in a Mega serial as a main character and Parni was also acting as the heroine. Parni was 25 years of young and beautiful lady. She was very giggle type of girl and not serious with anything. During acting in that serial Parni and Dipten came in touch to each other. She respected him very much and always tried to take advice from him for good acting.The serial ran for four years with great TRP and during this time they felt an attraction between them. They were acting as husband and wife with a big age difference and it was like their own life story. They fall in love. Dipten forgot about his family, he felt excitement in life as if could do everything. Parni also forgot about her friends, family and society. During seven or eight hours of shooting, they felt very happy . Whole of the day they couldn't stop thinking about each other. Their faces glow with a smile. Soon their love story spread out and became spicy news to others. People laughed and made gossips about them.Dipten's wife and daughters stopped talking to him. Parni's parents tried hard to make her understand but failed. First, it was not so serious for Parni but slowly Dipten became the most important part of her life. He was like a light in her life. He pleaded with his wife and daughters to forgive him and he wanted to live the rest of his life with Parni or will die. His devotional love for her made Parni mad at him. He gave huge alimony to his wife to make him free only for his love.

Ignoring all the boundaries they started living together with enormous love and happiness. Dipen always told her," I am grateful to God to have you in my life maybe I did some good work so I have got you".He had a desire to open a production house for the old artists who have lost their values. Two years of togetherness just went as a dream and Dipen fell sick suddenly, Parni couldn't save him. But after that incident, Parni's life changed. She stopped acting and became a producer with the motto to open a production house for her love. After a long fight, she opened DIPA which means light in the name of Dipten and Parni(DI+PA=DIPA). The endless love of Dipten gave her the courage to fulfil his wish and makes her grateful to him. His boundless love made her realise there is nothing in life beyond love.

CHAPTER TWENTY-FOUR

CONSCIENCE

Maloti Bera is now 80 years old. Lives in a room on the ground floor of the popular private hospital. Every day she visits the hospital for few hours. When she comes everyone like doctors, nurses, staffs all stand up and say her namaste. ' Maloti ma'. She feels very happy to hear the word' ma'. Once she was thirsty to hear it. she is not much educated and not so smart. She used to talk to the patients, wants to know if they feel any problems there. She is a very kind-hearted and well-behaved lady. Not only the patients she is very much aware of the patient's party also.

Jagadish Bera was a farmer with lots of land. His ancestors were farmers. Maloti and Jagadish never became parents. It was grief for them. In their village most of the people are farmers. There were not so many facilities in that village. One day when Jagadish became ill Maloti took him to a government hospital which is far away from their village. And then there was no private hospital in the village. The doctors suspected kidney failure. That government hospital had no modern equipment for dialysis. So after few days of suffering, he passed away. Then Maloti was55. This incident made her so remorse she thought to herself she will do something for the better treatment of the poor.

After few years she wished to build a private hospital on her land. So she donated all her land for the hospital. Only she kept one room for her. The B.D.O and the administration helped her to fulfil her wish. The villagers and some rich people helped her financially. It was named "Workers, Labourers Hospital". Now this private hospital is very popular for better treatment with less expanse for the poor and needy people. People know it as a cheap private hospital, few people know who is behind it? When it was formed then it was not so big slowly it becomes a great hospital. Once she was asked who inspired her to do this? She answered it was her conscience nothing else.

CHAPTER TWENTY-FIVE

DEVOTEE

Kalpana Desai was a nurse. She worked in a super speciality hospital in a different city . From her childhood she was very soft hearted.Once she read about the life of Florence Nightingal,whom people called 'The Lady With the Lamp" and she thought to herself that, one day she will be like her.Her dad was died when she was little.Her mom raised her two children with agony. She is a tailor.Kalpana and her younger brother Krish understood the pain of their mom. After ending class twelve she started reading B.Sc Nursing. It was four years course. She did very well in the final exam. And then she got the job as a nurse in that hospital. After getting job she thought now all will be good. First her mom was not agreed to let her go to a different city, but the salary was good and they really needed money as Krish wanted to study medical. So she went to join the hospital,there she lived in the hospital's hostel with many other nurses. Every month she used to send money to her mom and Krish started reading medical. After few months Kalpana requested her mom not to do so much hard work.

Everything was going smoothly. Most of the time Kalpana had to do her duty in the intensive care unit(icu) of the hospital. The patients of that department need extra care and Kalpana was very sympathetic to the patients and very skilled to take care of them. All the staffs ,doctors, nurses and the patients love her very much for her gentleness.Within few months she became very dear to all.Her hostel was very near to the hospital so most of the time she remained in the hospital and took great care of her patients.

She never behaved rudely like other nurses. The patients had a great trust on her and sometimes the patients party honoured her with some gifts. If there will be any problem Kalpana handled it perfectly,she always remained in smiling face.So all called her, "Lady, the solution to all problems".

She used to go two times to her own house in a year for one month. This time after coming from her home one day when it was her night duty. Suddenly a fire broke out from a short circuit in the basement. The spread of the fire was aided by the illegal storage of flammable materials in the basement of the hospital. When Kalpana knew about the fire she didn't run to save her life but she started saving the patients. Before her death she saved 39 patients. But she died when she was trying to help the another one. That night Kalpana could easily save her life but she only thought about her duty as a nurse, and the lady failed to solve,how to remain alive? Actually she was a devotee to her profession.